Life Under the Sea

Sea Stars

by Cari Meister

Bullfrog Books

Ideas for Parents and Teachers

Bullfrog Books give children practice reading informational text at the earliest levels. Repetition, familiar words, and photo labels support early readers.

Before Reading

- Discuss the cover photo with the class. What does it tell them?
- Look at the picture glossary together. Read and discuss the words.

Read the Book

- "Walk" through the book and look at the photos. Let the child ask questions.
- Read the book to the child, or have him or her read independently.

After Reading

- Prompt the child to think more. Ask: What do you think a sea star feels like? Which sea star in the book do you think is the most beautiful? Why?

Bullfrog Books are published by Jump!
5357 Penn Avenue South
Minneapolis, MN 55419
www.jumplibrary.com

Library of Congress Cataloging-in-Publication Data
Meister, Cari.
  Sea stars / by Cari Meister.
    p. cm. -- (Bullfrog books. Life under the sea)
  Summary: "This photo-illustrated nonfiction story for young readers describes the body parts of sea stars and how they are adapted to find food in the ocean. Includes picture glossary"--Provided by publisher.
  Includes bibliographical references and index.
  ISBN 978-1-62031-012-0 (hardcover : alk. paper)
  1. Starfishes--Juvenile literature. I. Title.
QL384.A8M45 2013
593.9'3--dc23
                                                    2012008430

Series Editor: Rebecca Glaser
Series Designer: Ellen Huber
Production: Chelsey Luther

Photo Credits: Dreamstime.com, 3b, 24; Getty Images, 6-7, 12-13, 16-17, 19, 23bl, 23tr; NHPA/Photoshot, 13; Photo Researchers, 21; Shutterstock, cover, 1, 3t, 4, 5, 8, 14b, 20, 22, 23tl, 23mr; SuperStock, 9, 10-11, 15, 18-19, 22inset, 23ml, 23br; Veer, 14t

Printed in the United States of America at Corporate Graphics in North Mankato, Minnesota
7-2012/ PO 1125
10 9 8 7 6 5 4 3 2 1

Table of Contents

Sea Stars Under the Sea

A sea star is hungry.
It is looking for food.

Sea stars cannot see.

How do they find food?

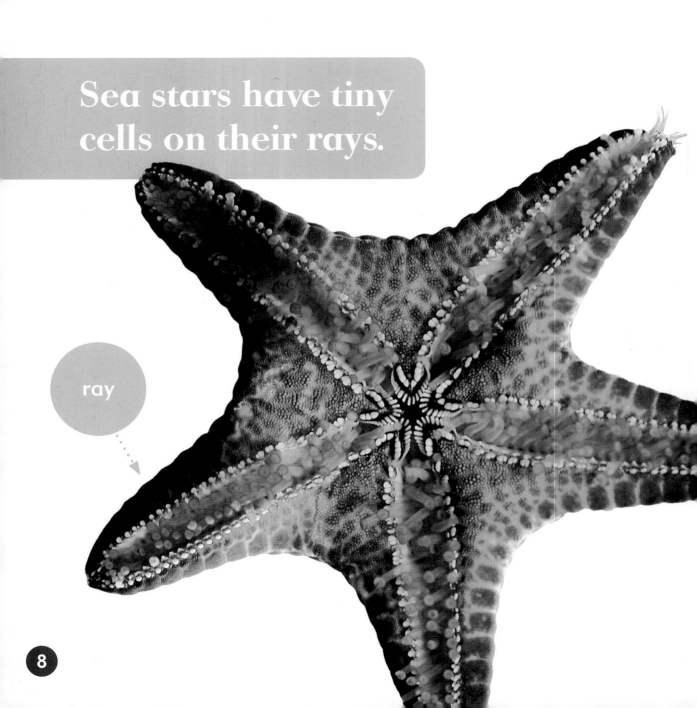

Sea stars have tiny
cells on their rays.

ray

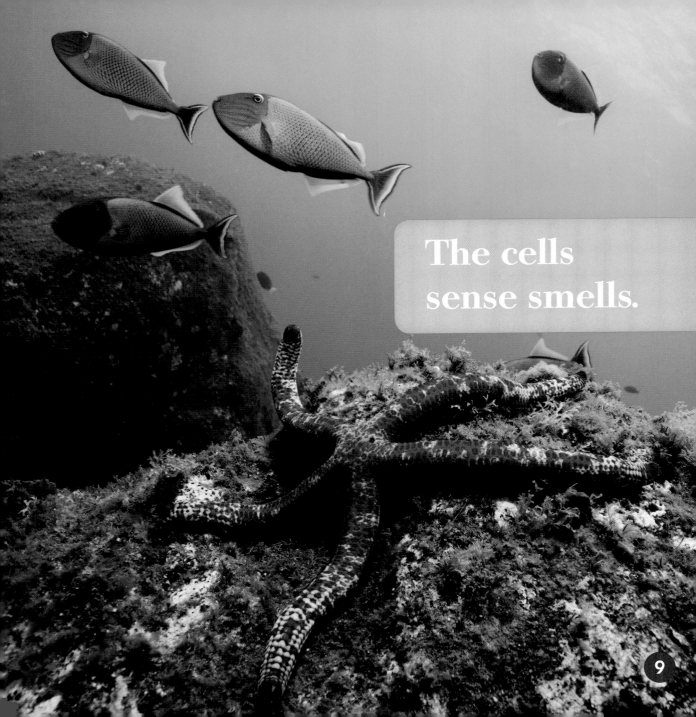

The cells
sense smells.

Sea stars have
hundreds
of tube feet.

They help sea
stars move.

Sea stars have
eye spots.

Eye spots sense
light and dark.

eye
spot

13

Watch out clams!

Watch out scallops!

Watch out oysters!
A sea star is near.

It might eat you!

The sea star hunches
over a clam.

Its tube feet stick
to the shells.

19

The sea star pulls and pulls.
The clam opens!
Now the sea star feasts.

Parts of a Sea Star

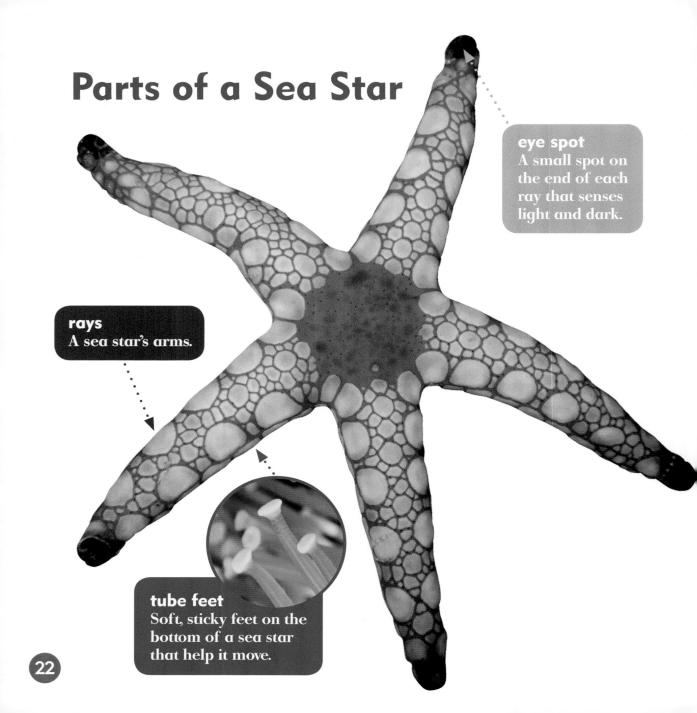

eye spot
A small spot on the end of each ray that senses light and dark.

rays
A sea star's arms.

tube feet
Soft, sticky feet on the bottom of a sea star that help it move.

Picture Glossary

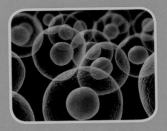

cells
A part of the body that can only be seen with a microscope.

oyster
A flat shellfish with two shells; pearls can grow in oysters.

clam
A shellfish with two shells that close tightly together.

scallop
A shellfish that has wavy, curved shells that open and close.

hunch
To round the body and bend over something.

sense
To feel, see, hear, smell, taste, or be aware of something.

Index

To Learn More

Learning more is as easy as 1, 2, 3.

1) Go to www.factsurfer.com

2) Enter "sea star" into the search box.

3) Click the "Surf" button to see a list of websites.

With factsurfer.com, finding more information is just a click away.